ADVANCE PRAISE FOR

It's Kina Hard Da' Cry: Art and Writings by Adults Incarcerated

"An amazing collection of writings and artwork. It's Kina Hard Da' Cry powerfully embraces the courage and spirit of its authors and doesn't hold back in saying what needs to be said."

—Dr. Richard J. White, Sheffield Hallam University, UK

"This powerful collection of voices educating us behind inhuman walls designed to create despair and hopelessness is a testament to the unyielding spirit of righteous defiance in the face of an unforgiving carceral culture."

—Dr. Peter McLaren, author of Pedagogy of Insurrection

"This beautiful collection shows the human cost of the prison-industrial complex and is inspirational reading for everyone fighting against the racist mass imprisonment in capitalist societies. These writings are a powerful reminder that, while there is a soul in prison, none of us are free."

—Dr. Will Boisseau,
Director of Administration, Institute for Critical Animal Studies

"Its Kina Hard to Cry is real, raw, and revolutionary. Its veins, sinew, and ink written by writers on the inside add depth and dimension to prison literature, a vastly underappreciated genre."

—Dr. Lea Lani Kinikini,
Chief Diversity Officer, Salt Lake Community College

"That the incarcerated are a large and growing population, intentionally sequestered and silenced by the joint state-corporate industrial complex, is all the more reason to seek such voices out and hear what they have to say. This collection gives numerous voices the exposure they deserve, to speak on why the prison industrial complex, based solely on coercion and domination, cannot be reformed but must be wholly transformed and abolished in the absolute."

—Nathan Poirier,
Director of Publicity, Institute for Critical Animal Studies

"Centering the voices of incarcerated individuals is essential to eliminate prisons and the school-to-prison pipeline. It's Kina Hard Da Cry provides space for these voices, making this collection an essential read for anyone committed to the abolition of the carceral state, and the creation of more just and compassionate communities."

—Dr. Scott Hurley,
Associate Professor, Identity Studies Department, Luther College

"A heart-wrenching poetry book from people who are decrying their experience "decaying in PrisneyLand," as one of its writers, Rusty Clark, says so powerfully. These poems give a glimpse into life on the inside: of broken family bonds, of children doing time on the outside, and agitating against the school-to-prison pipeline. For the novice, this is a book of raw stories from adults, who are as hurt as children, and share the violence of social death. Yet the system fails to break them."

—Dr. Mechthild Nagel, Professor, Philosophy, SUNY, Cortland

It's Kina Hard Da' Cry

Series Editors
Anthony J. Nocella II and Lea Lani Kinikini

Vol. 3

Edited by Save the Kids from Incarceration

It's Kina Hard Da' Cry

Art and Writings by Adults Incarcerated

New York - Berlin - Bruxelles - Chennai - Lausanne - Oxford

Library of Congress Cataloging-in-Publication Control Number: 2024047610

Bibliographic information published by the Deutsche Nationalbibliothek. The German National Library lists this publication in the German National Bibliography; detailed bibliographic data is available
on the Internet at http://dnb.d-nb.de.

Cover art designed and owned by Ricardo Levins Morales - https://www.rlmartstudio.com/

ISSN 2835-9275 (print)
ISSN 2835-9283 (online)
ISBN 9781636677361 (paperback)
ISBN 9781636677378 (ebook)
ISBN 9781636677385 (epub)
DOI 10.3726/b22419

Save the Kids from Incarceration (STKI) is a fully volunteer national grassroots organization dedicated to alternatives to and the end of incarceration of all youth and the school to prison pipeline.

Contact:

www.savethekidsgroup.org

poetrybehindthewalls@gmail.com

Published by Peter Lang Publishing Inc., New York, USA info@peterlang.com - www.peterlang.com

This publication has been peer reviewed.

DEDICATION

This book is dedicated to the friends and family of Fred Hampton, Mark Clark, Move, Breonna Taylor, George Floyd, Bernardo Palacios-Carbajal, Dillon Taylor, Bobby Duckworth, Cindreia Europe, Cody Belgard, Allen Nelson, Darrien Hunt, Bernardo Palacios-Carbajal, Sandra Bland, Michael Brown, Terrance Franklin, Chad Breinholt, Danielle Willard, Patrick Harmon, Oscar Grant, Amadou Diallo, Zane James, Dillon Taylor, Eric Garnder, Tamir Rice, Trayvon Martin, Freddie Gray Jr., Terrence Ledell Sterling, Bryan Pena Valencia. Tanisha Anderson, Yvette Smith, Miriam Carey, Shelly Frey, Darnisha Harris, Malissa Williams, Alesia Thomas, Shantel Davis, Rekia Boyd, Shereese Francis, Aiyana Stanley-Jones, Tarika Wilson, Kathryn Johnston, Alberta Spruill, Kendra James, and the many others killed because of police shootings.

THE STORY OF SAVE THE KIDS FROM INCARCERATION

Save the Kids from Incarceration emerged in the summer of 2009 out of Outdoor Empowerment (OE), a nonprofit established in 2005. Save the Kids National was established in August 2011.

Save the Kids from Incacceration from Incarceration is a nonprofit 501 c 3 national organization located in Utah.

In 2009, four African-American youth (Jason, Ali, Jarih, and Amound) in Hillbrook Juvenile Detention Facility chose "Save the Kids" and its mission, while participating in a group discussion about the need for an organization to keep them from being trapped in the juvenile justice system. They needed, as one kid stated, "to be saved instead of thrown away as trash." That statement speaks volumes.

Save the Kids from Incarceration does not claim to have all the answers, nor are we outsiders coming in to "save" anyone. We are individuals who have and had family members incarcerated in youth detention facilities and/or adult prisons and jails. We are made up of formerly incarcerated youth and adults, politicians, lobbyists, policymakers, judges, lawyers, detention staff and administration, youth advocates, teachers, religious leaders, and mentors.

PURPOSE STATEMENT

Save the Kids from Incarceration is a national grass-roots transformative justice organization dedicated to building a movement for alternatives to and the end of the school to prison pipeline and the policing, criminalizing, and incarcerating of all youth.

MISSION STATEMENT

Save the Kids from Incarceration through transformative justice, hip hop, and lowriders, advocates with and for justice-impacted BIYOC.

History

Save the Kids from Incarceration was founded in 2009 by four brilliant hopeful Black youth, Amoud, Jahri, Ali, and Jason, in a juvenile detention facility in New York to liberate and defend all systems impacted BIYOC.

Programs

Save the Kids from Incarceration has three BIYOC focused programs are all free, public, celebratory, and family-friendly and led by BIYOC to provide space and place for BIYOC voices and stories with partnerships between key agencies such as juvenile detention facilities, organizations, school districts, and colleges/universities.

When you become part of Save the Kids from Incarceration you: receive educational development, build your network, become part of a larger movement, and receive awareness-based merchandise that funds the organization.

The three programs are Transformative Justice Program, Hip Hop Studies Program, and Lowrider Studies Program.

1) Transformative Justice Program:

   (a) Alternatives to Violence Project (AVP) workshops (life skills and conflict transformation)
   (b) support group (basic needs and career support group)
   (c) education through action events (design and implement strategies to reduce ACE & Concentrated Disadvantage Impact)(d) Outreach and Stabilization (health and well-being)

2) Hip Hop Studies Program:

   (a) educational events (such as conferences, film screenings, lectures, workshops, and teach-ins)
   (b) community shows (such as poetry slams, Hip Hop shows, DJ battles, lowrider shows, and cyphers)
   (c) productions/publications (such as newsletters, journals, podcasts, videos, and books)

3) Lowrider Studies Program:

   (a) educational events (such as conferences, film screenings, lectures, workshops, and teach-ins)
   (b) community shows (such as poetry slams, Hip Hop shows, DJ battles, lowrider shows, and cyphers)
   (c) productions/publications (such as newsletters, journals, podcasts, videos, and books

TEN POINT PRINCIPLES

1. Save the Kids from Incarceration believes that all youth need support, love, and skills in order to achieve their goals.
2. Save the Kids from Incarceration believes that all youth are amazing and wonderful, no matter the actions they have committed.
3. Save the Kids from Incarceration makes a clear distinction between actions and kids; actions can be bad, but not kids.
4. Save the Kids from Incarceration is committed to promoting food justice for healthy sustainable living with youth because they are our future and if we do not help them, we will not have one.
5. Save the Kids from Incarceration believes in respecting all gender, ability, race, economic status, sexuality, religion, ethnicity, health, age, or nationality.
6. As a Hip Hop studies organization, Save the Kids from Incarceration works towards both social justice and the end of all forms of oppression, specifically the school-to-prison pipeline.
7. As an organization based on transformative justice principles, Save the Kids from Incarceration strives to promote and analyze alternatives to incarceration, such as community-based programs, rather than institutionalization.
8. Save the Kids from Incarceration believes in peace and nonviolence in resolving and transforming all conflicts.
9. Save the Kids from Incarceration rejects the stigma created by labeling and are inclusive in all of our activities.
10. Save the Kids from Incarceration promotes interdependence, that everyone in the community should work together in making a peaceful world and not to exclude anyone. Save the Kids from Incarceration will work with everyone and anyone in order to achieve that goal.

CONTENTS

FOREWORD

FRANK HERNANDEZ

On January 18, 2000, I received a letter from my brother, who at the time was in the Mark W. Stiles Unit, a Texas Department of Criminal Justice men's prison located near Beaumont, Texas. It was the first of many letters. And, while I was happy and grateful to receive these letters—and I received a lot of them—I always felt a pressing, unpleasant obligation to write him back.

I did write him back. But my letters got shorter while his letters got longer. He always had more to say to me than I must have had to say to him. I realize now that my letters to him, even if they were short, had a profound impact on his ability to detect hope and joy in a place where isolation and feelings of neglect are experienced every day and can permeate one's entire existence. For my brother, there was something about hearing his name yelled out loud when he was being told that he had mail. This announcement conveyed to other inmates the message that someone on the outside cared about him. I learned about the impact of my letters once my brother got out of prison. He told me about their importance. Knowing the impact of my letters, I wish now I would have sent more of them and devoted more time to them.

I still have all the letters my brother wrote (including the ones he wrote our mother). As I prepared to write the foreword to this book, I began to read and re-read his letters for inspiration. I noticed a few things about the letters; they were always deeply reflective. My brother has always been a deep thinker, reflecting profoundly about almost everything in his life. But his reflections in the prison letters felt different. In these reflections he would contemplate his entire existence. A single comment would manage to draw everything together, ranging from childhood memories to his early adulthood relationships to how he made sense of his current situation. These were not the "I wish I had not made this bad decision" types of letters. These were letters in which he accepted full responsibility for his actions and the consequences that came with those actions. In this regard, I am keenly aware that prison offers one lots of time to be reflective, hence his long letters to me and my mother.

I also noticed that his letters were written like personal essays, like well-thought-out prose. I often thought that, if needed, his essays could easily be turned into poetry or song. Although I did not notice it at the time, his letters are remarkably spiritual in nature. They are not about forgiveness or being "saved"; they are my brother's testimonials about his past, his present, his calling in life, and the next steps in his journey.

He would include a Bible verse now and again, yet the letters were never about the Bible verses in themselves; rather, they were about how the Bible verses were playing themselves out in his own life—in prison. His letters also contained lots of references to our mother, whom he has always called his "angel." In the final analysis, the letters inspired me. They made me think about my own challenges, including those I had faced as a full-time school administrator. I asked myself how my own challenges matched up to the challenges that my brother had faced during his prison term. As I re-read his letters, it dawned on me that they constituted his only outlet with the outside world. These days, all of us on the outside know how easy it is to send a quick email, text message, or Tweet. But let us never forget the unmatchable value of the handwritten word. And let us never fail to appreciate the powerful emotional connection that establishes itself between a prisoner and his or her loved ones on the outside. The letters that I received were my brother's only way to communicate his successes, challenges, fears, frustrations, failures, and pain, with me. The prison system made a direct telephone call too expensive, and a simple picture sent over email nearly impossible. Letter writing was my brother's only feasible way of expressing himself to his closest connections in the world.

This is why "It's Kina Hard Da' Cry: Art and Writing by Adults Incarcerated" is critical to our understanding of American society. Incarcerated youth and adults are far from an insignificant segment of the U.S. population, and they deserve a way to express themselves so that their creativity and their spoken word become public—so that their voices are heard. The book that you are reading right now is divided into distinct categories of writing. However, the drama and indeed the trauma in these stories are real. Love and discontent flow from the words, regardless of how they've been structured. The book offers us an opportunity to hear the voices that are often muffled and rarely expressed. I encourage you to read this book with the love and compassion with which its authors endowed its contents.

My brother today is out of prison and clean. I cherish the moments when he calls me on my cell phone and asks me to listen to a new song he just composed or a new poem he just wrote. I make a real effort to listen carefully and thoughtfully, and to be the ear that hears everything he has to say—because he, and so many others like him, deserve to be heard.

PREFACE

JONATHAN PAUL

The one thing you never forget when you enter past the prison door is the echoing sounds of shutting doors, the sounds of the keys rattling as the guards walk around the cell, the loud yelling of other prisoners, and the echoing of all the noises that bounce off the cold walls and floors. The sense of loneliness permeates your body and your thoughts even though you are surrounded by other inmates. The sense of danger and fear and the yearning to survive always dominate your thoughts and feelings.

As time goes by and one adjusts to this new reality, the sinking feeling of being away from those you love becomes overwhelming and depressing. One can make some connections and maybe a friend while locked up, however trusting others can be a struggle. When others approach you the sense of what might or could happen to your physical and mental self is always in the back of your mind. Navigating daily life is a chore and can be stressful. Your well-being is always like finding your way through a maze that seems to have no exit.

In many ways, the only way to keep yourself sane is to make a routine for yourself, whether exercising in the yard, reading books, educating yourself, writing to loved ones on the outside or, like in this book, writing poetry. Writing, whether letters or poetry, is a way of coping and a way of expressing your feelings in a reality where feelings can only be suppressed. But in finding yourself and dealing with your emotions you are basically on your own. In many ways, the dominant feeling that is expressed in prison is anger and hatred. Your other emotions remain locked inside you just as you are locked behind walls and fences of razor wire.

When doing time, one has a choice on *how* to do your time. You can sleep it away and drown in your sadness, or you can find a way to connect with yourself and find ways to express your emotions. For myself, I did two things: I wrote letters and I exercised. I ran around the yard six days a week to push out my frustrations and my anger, the razor-wire fences always reminding me that I could only run around a track in circles. I did, however, feel some sort of personal freedom. I always knew my time there was finite and one day I would walk free; however, time that we take for granted in the free world was dominating my daily life. Hours, days, weeks, and months seemed longer, seemed more consuming, and felt like I was slogging through a swamp just wanting to get to dry land.

I did, however, find myself dreaming about being in places I would take for granted when I was outside the walls. I would dream of walking through the woods, hearing the birds singing, and feeling the grasses rub against my hands. I would write my thoughts in letters to my friends and supporters, and in some ways it would increase my frustration but also a sense of peace.

Since I went to prison for political activities in both the environmental and animal rights movements, I was lucky to have friends and supporters who would write to me. There were so many letters that it was impossible for me to write everyone back individually so I set up a system where I would write one letter, send it to my sister, who would do a bulk mailing to everyone on my list. By writing one group letter I could focus on conveying the message rather than trying to make sure to complete hundreds of letters to express my gratitude for their support and love. I would write about my feelings and concerns, and would also be able to allow friends, supporters, and families to know how their support was keeping me strong and keeping that constant emptiness, I was feeling a little bit better.

Although I did not write poetry, I would write about missing nature, missing sitting next to a forest creek and hearing the gurgle of water slipping over the rocks while feeling the sunshine on my face. I wrote about one special place I used to spend time in the years before, in the Umpqua forest in Oregon, where two mountain lakes were surrounded by ancient forest. The water was so clear you could see to the bottom of the alpine lakes and the trees were so large I felt so small and so insignificant. These thoughts of this wild and beautiful place were poetry for my soul. It always gave me hope that someday soon, I would be able to experience the wonders of nature and the healing of my most inner self.

Making the best of your stay in prison can only result in a positive life when you are released back into society. Allowing your creative side to come out when you are locked up is a healthy, positive way to express yourself and be in touch with your inner feelings. The key to all this, however, is to be able to hold onto this as you re-enter society and move on with your life, putting the fence and razor wire in the distant past.

"It's Kina Hard Da' Cry: Art and Writing by Adults Incarcerated", edited by Save the Kids from Incarceration, centers an extremely marginalized group of people: prisoners. This book is an important, powerful, and needed book within the realm of social justice, critical criminology, racial justice, and prisoner support. This book speaks to me on many levels as a former prisoner. The words in the book are from people doing life in prison to a few years. There are many brilliant minds society can learn from behind the walls. This is your chance to learn and listen to someone you might not normally be able to communicate with.

ACKNOWLEDGMENTS

We would like to thank all the youth who contributed their writing and art. This project would not exist without each and every one of you. Thank you for sharing your voices and personal experiences.

We would like to thank all the volunteers in Save the Kids from Incarceration who made this project possible. This includes the Save the Kids from Incarceration volunteers who coordinate youth workshops every week in juvenile detention centers across the United States.

Thank you to Ricardo Levins Morales, artist and activist, for contributing a piece of your invaluable artwork. Morales' artwork is featured on the cover of this book. Thank you for your long dedication to social justice through art.

Thank you to the editorial board for your diligent support, effort, and commitment toward publishing *Wisdom Behind the Walls.*

We would like to thank Frank Hernandez for writing the forward and Jonathan Paul for writing the Preface.

Finally, we thank all of you who support Save the Kids from Incarceration and by doing so contribute to the ongoing existence of the *Wisdom Behind the Walls* book series.

POETRY FROM ADULTS INCARCERATED

"NO WORDS"

Written: 9-3-2006 By: Rev. David E. [illegible] Sr. © [illegible] Music
(About Childhood Abuse)

I, just can't seem to remember,
Others, just can't forget
But, I don't know which is worse.
Oh..., get outta my head, No, you can't stay
Oh no I can't say, Time's moving on
I've grown away, my heart is strong now
No you can't take it away,
Minds move on, hearts mend, spirits grow.
Times move on, I've grown away
my heart is strong now
No you can't take it away
I, ain't got no words to say
No, you can't stay.
I just can't get it outta my head
I just want to get on with my life
No. I don't wanna talk about it.
I just need to love you, Your love can save me.
Your love can save me (Whoa, Hey)
Gotta leave it all behind ( )
Baby just love me, as I am.
Just can't get it outta my head
Don't wanna talk about it
Just want you to love me

NO WORDS

REV. DAVID E. ROSE SR.
Eastern Correctional Institute, Maryland

I, just can't seem to remember,
Others, just can't forget
Well, I don't know which is worse.
Oh. . ., get outa my head, No, you can't stay
Oh no I can't say, Time's moving on
I've grown away, my heart is strong now
No you can't take it away,
Minds move on, heart mends, spirits grow.
Times move on, I've grown away
My heart is strong now
No you can't take it away
I ain't got no words to say
No, you can't stay.
I just can't get it outa my head
I just want to get on with my life
No. . . I don't wanna talk about it
I just want to love you, Yeah Love can save me.
Yeah Love can save me (Whoo—Hoo)
Gotta Leave it all behind (Whoo—Hoo)
Baby just love me, as I am.
Just can't get it outa my head
Don't wanna talk about it
Just want you to Love one
Just want to Love you

"SONG FOR MOM"

Written 3-17-[illegible] Additional lyrics 3-28-2011
by Rev. "David E." [illegible], Sr. © [illegible] Music"

Crazy I hope you don't mind if I borrow
a few notes.
Singing Bird forgive me for my past.
I know you do" I love you so much
and miss you too. Hello again, it's me!
Don't worry Mama, these walls can't hold
me here. I am always with you, you are.
Beloved Woman/Arrow Annie/Sadaye.
Mama I hope you don't mind
if I stick around a while
don't worry Mama, I'll meet you
in the next world, I won't be late
There won't be no more pain, oh no.
there won't be no pain. Wait for
me Mama, I'll see you there
Mama I'm coming home, I'll see you soon
You're always in my heart, you
taught me so much. Honor, love, trust
Hold you in my heart always in my
thoughts!

SONGS FOR MOM

REV. DAVID E. ROSE SR.
Eastern Correctional Institute, Maryland

Ozzy I hope you don't mind if I borrow a few notes. . .
Singing Bird forgive me for my past.
I know you do! I love you so much
and miss you too! Hello again, it's me!
Don't worry momma, these walls can't hold
me here. I am always with you, you are.
Beloved woman / Arrow Annie / Sadayi.
Mama I hope you don't mind if I stick around a while
don't worry momma, I'll meet you
in the next world, I won't be late.
There won't be no more pain, Ah no..
There won't be no pain, Wait for
me momma, I'll see you there!
Momma I'm coming home, I'll see you soon.
Your always in my heart, you
taught me so much. Honor, love, trust,
hold you in my Heart always in my thought.

AS YOU NAVIGATE, UNDERSTAND AND
UNDERESTIMATE, IF YOU'RE LIVING LIFE
DRIVING DOWN THE WRONG HIGHWAY,
I WAS GIVEN THE CHANCE TO SHOW
WITH A SPECIAL HANDSHAKE...

CHANCE TO CELEBRATE,
LIKE EVERYONE THAT [illegible]
SAME FATE...

SO LISTEN CLOSELY WHEN I SAY,
THE [illegible] CAN MAKE MISTAKES.

EVERYONE

EDUARDO TOLENTINO JR.
Imperial County Jail, CA

Any person can make mistakes,
But listen closely because time
Cannot be replaced...

It will not hesitate, as years pass by
You see it's real not fake,
Find the proper balance in life so your
Path can illuminate...

It's never too late,
The answer key is for you to make...

As you navigate, understand and don't
Underestimate, if your living life to fast
Driving down the wrong highway,
I was given the chance to provide you
With a special handbrake...

Before you crash and never get the
Chance to celebrate,
Like everyone that didn't have the
Same fate...

So listen closely when I say,
That any person can make mistakes.

THE FALLACY OF JUSTICE

TREVOR A. BROWN
Faribault Prison, MN

Recently, after having been incarcerated at level four and five prisons for the past twenty years I was transferred to a level three, medium custody, facility. The route that was taken just so happened to pass through many of the cities and towns I formerly hung out in during my adolescent years, and also where my crime occurred. As the bus trucked along and my eyes absorbed everything in their view I slowly began to process what I was seeing and realized that I no longer recognized the place I once called home. Everything was different. Nothing was like I remembered. But more importantly, I was different. Psychologically. Emotionally. Spiritually. Socially. And now I even had a political point of view. I was no longer a lost and reckless eighteen year old boy that got himself sent to prison with a life sentence but an educated, responsible, and mature thirty eight year old man. This sobering reality promoted me to take measure of the justness of my plight in the context of crime and punishment in America.

In the field of criminology the underlying theory behind sentencing someone to some duration of confinement is deterrence. Therefore, the premise of this concept as I understand it is that by merely sentencing me to a term of imprisonment it is supposed to deter others contemplating engaging in some form of criminal conduct.

TWO TRUTHS AND A LIE

By Maurice L. Graham (March 2009)

A.

In·jus·tice (in-jus'tis), n. 1. Violation of the rights of others. 2. An act that is not fair, honest, or moral.

I am a very blessed person. I may not have everything in life, but I have access to clean water, healthy food, and most importantly, time with those I love.

My nieces are girly-girls: sweet, kind, brilliant, and unimaginably beautiful.

***

B.

Injustice is a lotus flower floating atop a pool of sky-tinted water at the base of a bodhi tree. Dewdrops cradled in its petals bow away from the sunlight, refracting sweet-scented prisms into the eye of dawn.

I used to have dreams where my teeth shattered. This bothered me for years until one day I came across a book about dreams that explained how it meant I was having premonitions of suffering. I told my mother, who was raised by an Arkansas Pentecostal, and she told me God isn't cruel enough to give me a vision without giving me a chance to do something about it. "There is nothing that you can't fix if you know the problem," she said. "Don't ever be afraid of your dreams, just do what needs to be done and things'll be okay."

III.

Little girls have more insight than grown men. Early on, when I began fancying myself as an author, I found I liked writing every style that came my way. From time to time people would ask me what I considered as my genre. I would be paralyzed with indecision because there are several I enjoy, and ultimately the answer would spill out something like 'Oh, I like to write speculative fiction, some poetry, a little memoir, westerns, horror, romance, and on occasion

TWO TRUTHS AND A LIE

MAURECE L. GRAHAM
Faribault Prison, MN

A

I.

In jus tice (in jus'tis), n. 1. Violation of the rights of others. 2. An act that is not fair, honest, or moral.

II.

I am a very blessed person. I may not have everything in life, but I have access to clean water, healthy food, and most importantly, time with those I love.

III.

My nieces are girly-girls: sweet, kind, brilliant, and unimaginably beautiful.

***

B

I.

Injustice is a lotus-flower floating atop a pool of sky-tinted waters at the base of a bodhisattva tree. Dewdrops cradled in its petals bow away from the sun-light, refracting sweet-scented prisms into the eye of dawn.

II.

I used to have dreams where my teeth shattered. This bothered me for years until one day I came across a book about dreams that explained how it meant I was having premonitions of suffering. I told my mother, who was raised in Arkansas Pentecostal, and she told me God isn't cruel enough to give me a vision without giving me a chance to do something about it. "There is nothing that you can't fix if you know the problem," she said. "Don't ever be afraid of your dreams, just do what needs to be done and things'll be okay."

III.

Little girls have more insight than grown men. Early on, when I began fancying myself as an author, I found I liked writing every style that came my way. From time to time people would ask me what I considered as my genre. I would be paralyzed with indecision because there are several I enjoy, and ultimately the answer would spill out something like "Oh, I like to write speculative fiction, some poetry, a little memoir, westerns, horror, romance, and on occasion historical fiction." This answer sounded impressively expansive to me and served me well until I volunteered to write a story for my seven-year-old niece. I asked her, "What kind of story would you like me to write, Princess?" "Hmmm...," she purred, "could you write me a comedy?"

***

C

I.

Injustice is not funny, it is real. For some, it extends from slavery, and for others, classism, sexism, xenophobia, and eugenics. Many of us are like GMOs and find ourselves amenable to whatever label the occasion requires.

II.

I saw a bodhisattva once, just after I died but before I came back to life and levitated. He didn't call himself that, in fact he told me he was me, and, as I recall, he did look just like me, but that isn't the main thing. The main thing is that he taught me about justice. He let me see all people need love, and then reminded me it's just us.

III.

My niece wears a t-shirt of mugshots of her fellow third-graders, and also marches in school-to-prison-pipeline rallies. She has a face color of powdered mocha, perennially unruly sandy-brown hair, and a smile that is one part post-toddler adorable, and one part I-am-farther-along-on-this-journey-than-you-imagine. I found out she was going to be born right in the middle of a rant. "Prison and profits can never go hand-in-hand," I was saying, when my mother piped in, "Your baby sister is going to have a baby." My rant was epic so I continued. "Money trumps advocacy every time, and you will never get corrections to work on behalf of the public safety in areas where public safety clashes with the interests of their shareholders." Then my jaw stopped working, and passed the baton to my ear ducts.

***

D

I.

Injustice should not be compared to lotus flowers or bodhisattva trees beside calm pools of water. It is not like the *Lotus Sutra* that advises how mindfulness of compassion can transform the fires that are about to burn us into cool, clear lotus lake; it is nothing like any bodhisattva tree, who's branches extend from a base liquid consciousness, of consciousness full of understanding, care, and love. Injustice is maddeningly unfair. Injustice should be seen like one sees a person who works hard to get a twenty-five cent pay raise only to lose seven thousand dollars in child care assistance. Injustice should bring to mind an absentee dad from an impoverished family who finally gets it together and dies of cancer before he makes a difference at home. Injustice should be compared to a shadow behind a little girl's eyes when she finds out her mother has full blown AIDS and her father has lost his mind.

II.

I find myself with little time between dreams, but on those occasions I try and make sense of the world and its contradictions. For instance, I live in one of the most powerful and wealthiest nations in recorded history with a long literary tradition. Authors like Alexis DE Tocqueville taught me that the "true" measure of any society lay in how it treats its prisoners. Inspired, one night I researched prisons in America and found: Two hundred seventy-four billion dollars annually are spent nationwide on the maintenance of incarceration. Over two million human beings are acknowledged to be under local, state, and federal confinement, including eighty thousand minors held in juvenile residential facilities, thirteen percent of whom are girls. Four million seven hundred thousand people are on parole or probation. Two thousand five hundred seventy-four juveniles in the United States are sentenced to die in prison via life without parole. Sixty-six million people overall have arrest records, and police have carried out more than a quarter billion arrests in the past twenty years. Per capita and overall there are more people either sentenced to death or incarcerated in the "land of the free" than in any other nation on the planet. I don't know if my teeth shattered that night but I dreamt again. "*Dukka*," said Kwan Yin, "*but you can change it.*"

III.

My niece has a knack for popping out with odd flashes of sophistication during the most mundane conversations. Our last phone call was typical. "Uncle," she said, "when are you coming home?" "When the lady with the computerized voice at the end of our call gets strangled in a cold, dark alley." "I'm going to help you get her. Then will you take me surfing?" "Princess. I'm going to take you surfing so much you're going to transform into sea foam." "Can I transform into a narwhale instead?" "Uh, sure. Why a narwhale?" "Because they're almost extinct and now everyone who sees them thinks they're special."

***

E

I.

Injustice is a bridge to nobody, an edifice to some, and an impediment to all.

II.

Avalokiteshvara is a bodhisattva that looks upon the world with crying eyes. Some who study the sutras say she is emblematic of great empathy, but I had an ipiphany and found out that she is simply incarcerated. *Ipiphany*: it is not an *e*piphany, where something comes to you, it is the opposite, where no one comes to you, as in "*prisoners don't have* epiphanies, *they have* i*piphanies, because no one ever comes to them.*" The easiest way is to remember that *e*piphanies deal with *things* and *i*piphanies deal with *people*. Ask any mother with a son or daughter in a far off prison, and she will explain it to you in greater detail.

III.

My sister-in-law abandoned my niece while prostituting to pay for her mental health problems. She was working-class generation X who came of age before Obamacare and instead of Lithium she had to visit a local drug outlet to treat her illness. The crack she was prescribed cost more than her 9-to-5 could afford, and after being beaten and left for dead one day she awoke in the hospital to the discovery that a) she would live; and b) she had AIDS. While she recovered, her daughter—my niece—was a toddler and left wandering the streets about one thousand miles from any family.

***

F

I.

Injustice is not always clear cut. Not everyone was incarcerated with an airtight alibi that the right lawyer can discover. DNA doesn't save those who weren't accused of anything requiring a blood test. Some people's actions were misinterpreted. Some people take lie detector tests to show that they really are innocent, not knowing that the prosecutors will hide this information like they hid embarrassing witnesses before trial. Some people who are innocent will spend decades behind bars, never get exonerated, and upon release live out the rest of their lives as anonymous, impoverished felons.

II.

I was raised believing I was part Hebrew but when I died my father's face was on the Sphinx. He turned to me and smiled, and a cousin and a brother showed up as well. This was before I found out that the three of them had a cancer, one from a childhood injury, the others from alcohol and cocaine respectively. I came back to life that day, and my Sphinx-faced father died nine years later from survivable cancer but unsurvivable lack of health insurance. By then I knew my nieces had no parents, I was on the dean's list in college, I looked upon the world with crying eyes. But I had also begun having *Ipiphanies* in a place where no one dared dream.

III.

Little girls are important. I have more than one niece, and they constantly ask me who my favorite is. There are three who are sisters, two who were found, and all of them think about the one who wasn't. When I answer their questions, I keep Her in mind, and hope She hears me. "Think of yourselves like car wheels. If even one of you is missing, it's impossible to go on." They are smart little girls, and they understand. I am a grown man, and I do not, even though it came from my lips.

***

G

I.

Injustice keeps father from their first loves, mothers from their first homes, daughters from their first dates and sons from their first proms. Injustice is a selfish lotus flower that floats atop storm-deepened waters, its blossoms drinking in crystalline shards of sunlight and warmth while everything beneath it drown.

II.

I am a grown man. I am in prison. My teeth do not shatter anymore because I do not dream. This is my second death, dying was my first. I realized I was wrong, and the sphinx made four with cancer.

III.

My niece was arrested at twelve years old, but couldn't be convicted because she wasn't fourteen. The prosecutors waited two years, and then sent her to jail anyways. They did not ask if she a mother with AIDS or a father with mental illness. They did not check to see if she would have a home if her grandmother did not live from her latest stroke. They did not think of her sisters. I talked to the lawyers over the phone from prison, told them about restorative justice and alternatives to incarceration, recited to them facts about the failures of retribution-based punishments and the successes of community-based interventions. They listened while the lawyer got paid, but when our healthcare-and-prison-leeched funds ran out, nobody cared. She was locked up, and now her sister is one of three, with the other two missing.

Key

A. I & III (T) [I am thankful for my blessings, but none of those reasons in the 2nd statement are true]

B. I & III (T) [See D]

C. II & III (T) [He never called himself a bodhisattva]

D. I & III (T) [I don't dream much, and I have never knowingly carried out a conversation with Kwan Yin]

E. I & III (T) [I don't really have Ipiphanies because I get visits about twice a year, which is two too many to have an Ipiphany]

F. I & III (T) [To say *no one* dares dream is an obvious exaggeration]

G. I & III (T) [I have some dreams]

I WON IN A TRIAL WHERE MANY HAVE LOST,
WHERE NO FORM OF CURRENCY CAN PAY THE COST.

WHOSE IT FOR?" AND "WHY CARE?"

TWO QUESTIONS I ANSWER DAILY,
I ASPIRE TO INFLUENCE THE MISUNDERSTOOD
VARYING IN AGE WITHOUT ENVY.

PERHAPS A MOVE TO ADDRESS A NATION IN DISTRESS,

EMER

THEN I'LL BE LOOKING OUT MY WINDOWS AND ASSESS,
THIS EXPERIENCE WAS NEEDED SO MY
VIEW CAN BECOME THE BEST.

TEACHER IS LIFE, AND NOW I GLADLY

THIS IS MY VIEW, JUST IN CASE I FORGOT
MENTION.

MY VIEW

EDUARDO TOLENTINO JR.
Imperial County Jail, CA

I won in a trial where many have lost,
Where no form of currency can pay the cost.

"Whose it for?" and "why care?"

Those two questions I answer daily,
As I aspire to influence the misunderstood;
Varying in age without envy.

Perhaps a move to address a nation in distress,
Can be declaring a national public health
Emergency and the problem caress.

Until then I'll be looking out my windows and assess,
That this experience was needed so my
View can become the best.

The teacher is life, and now I gladly
Pay attention,
This is my view, just in case I forgot
To mention.

1.) AFTER ALL THE DRAMA, THAT 've BEEN THROUGH, HAVING A BAD DAY SIMPLY "Will not" DO.

2.) I HAD TO ELEVATE MY HUSTLE TO SURVIVE "Legit." BECAUSE DOIN' life in the PEN. CAN Kill YOU QUICK.

3.) I Gotta TELL YOU the "TRUTH", I CANT DO NO LYIN', YOU DONT WANNA GET RICH, & THEN DIE TRYIN'.

4.) A TRUE HUSTLER ASKS "WHAT DO I HAVE TO LOSE"? HOW BAD DO <u>YOU</u> WANT IT? GET UP... MOVE!

5.) THERES NO LUGGAGE RACK ON A HEARSE, It AINT the things THAT YOU OWNED. ITS THE LOVE THAT YOU SHARE, the EXPERIENCES THAT YOU'VE KNOWN.

6.) I Love it when I HEAR THEM HATERS HATE'N. "I LOVE YOU All". MY MOTIVATION.

7.) IN THE GAME OF LIFE, YOU WILL ADVANCE, NEVER LET A ROOKIE KNOCK YOU OFF YOUR STANCE.

8.) "START" somethin', "BREAK" somethin', "SAVE" somethin', I've DONE EM' All, & I GOT BACK UP, AFTER EACH FALL.

9.) THE MOST DANGEROUS PERSON AINT JUST WISE FROM THE STREET. THEY GOT THE WISDOM OF GOD, SO DONT MESS w/ME.

10.) LIFES MESSED UP, & THEN YOUR GONE, SO BUCKLE UP & PUT YOUR HELMET ON.

11.) IT WASNT HARD TO CONVINCE THE STREETS, THAT I'M A "G". BUT its HARD TO CONVINCE THE WARDEN, ABOUT THE "NEW" ME.

12.) People NEVER REMEMBER All THE TIMES YOU SAID "YES", OR HOW YOU BEEN "KIND". BUT THAT ONE TIME YOU SAID... "NO" is WHAT STUCK IN THEIR MIND.

13.) BEIN' MAD AT THE WORLD JUST WONT HELP YOU SON. But GET "REALLY" MAD AT THE "Ri GS, & THEN YOU'VE WON.

14.) YOU CANT IMPRESS EVERYONE, SO DONT EVEN TRY, JUST Roll w/THE ONES WHO STICK BY YOUR SIDE..

After all the drama that I've been through, having a bad day simply "will not" do.

I had to elevate my hustle to survive "legit." Because doin life in the pen. Can kill you quick.

I gotta tell you the "truth," I can't do no lyin; you don't wanna get rich, & die tryin.

A true hustla asks "what do I have to lose?" "how bad do you want it?" Get up. . . move!

There's no luggage rack on a hearse, It ain't the things that you owned. It's the love that you share, the experi-ences that you've known.

I love it when I hear them haters haten. "I love you all," my motivation.

In the game of life, you will advance, never let a rookie knock you off your stance.

"Start" somethin, "break" somethin, "save" somethin, I've done em all. And I get back up, after each fall.

The most dangerous person ain't just wise from the street. They got the wisdom of god, so don't mess with me.

Lifes messed up, & then your gone, so buckle up & put your helmet on.

It wasn't hard to convince the streets, that I'm a "G." But it's hard to convince the warden, about the "new" me. People never remember all the times you said "yes," or how you been "kind." But that one time you said. . . "no" is what stuck in their mind.

Bein mad at the world just won't help you son. But get "really" mad at the "right" things, & then you've won. You can't impress everyone, so don't even try, just roll with the ones who stick by your side.

When you start comin up, a lot of people will talk down. That's all they'll ever have, "they belong" on the ground. Watch how your friends treat you, do they treat others the same? If they treat others messed up, then you might be part of their game.

Youngsta's think they know all there is to know. But they don't realize how "much" there is to know, just goes to show.

The last time you were sick & thought you were dyin did the feelin not pass? Life always gets better, if not you "would" have.

Respect for respect, yes ma'am, yes sir. They'll treat you "the same," did this thought not occur.

Stop askin for things, don't no one owe you nothin. Now "earn" your keep, go out & get something!

A player don't lie to his gal, she gone know the deal. If you sneak'n, then you cheat'n, naw fa real.

In the game of life, these words ring true, spectators, commentators & critics don't get the trophies, only the players do.

The people below you, remember them too, cause it's the people above you, that creates the envy in you.

If I seem "square" to you now, it's because I've been through the war. I've come full "circle," & the lessons were raw.

We tend to spit out the good advice that we're served. Remember medicine doesn't taste good, that's my word. It's true, no man can be great alone, you're only "great" when good people let it be known.

Money creates options, not happiness. That comes from "peace" have you met god yet?

A "gangsta" brings hurt & pain. A "gangster" will show love, "peace" he'll try to maintain.

A "nerd" talks about everything, the in's & out's. A "geek" actually gets it done, no doubt. (you may replace "nerd" with "boy" & "geek" with "man.")

I've left more "behind," than most will ever "gain." When you realize it, & your sincere, you'll understand I'm talking about "shame."

I've been "your age," you "ain't been" mine, sit down son, pay attention one time.

Early to bed, early to rise, 16-hrs a day is how I get mines. When doin biz with someone, & they say "gash will come quick," get out of the deal, ain't no such thing, they try'n to be slick.

A rich man losin everything will take his pride, but ain't no shame in the poor man try'n to survive.

"Freak" / "go-getter" / "wifey" are the "3" on my list, but if you're all of the above honey, that would be my wish. Old friends will try to pull you back down in time. Some-times cuttin loss is necessary to advance your grind. A bullet will hit you "before" you hear the sound of the shot. Don't let it be too late "before" you realize what you've lost.

Slow motion & low profile is better than it could be. "No motion" & "no profile" sounds a lot like "dead" to me. When you gamble in life, your takin a risk. Hustlers don't

lose what they "ain't got" in their fist.

I had to learn how to "act," let me speak truth, the role that I've played, I had to make due.

Do it yourself, even if you gotta fight. You gotta get your hands dirty if you want it done right.

Try spendin ½ the time on yourself, than you do worry'n about others. You gotta get yourself right first to truly help your sisters & brothers.

Son, wear your name like designer clothes. Cause people can spot fugazi if it's real it shows.

If you rest too long, you might fall asleep, keep it movin along, eyes open, there's a lot to see.

You might get some points with the popular vote. But it's "respect for respect," don't confuse them both.

If you were in a room & everyone threw their problems on the floor, you'd pick yours back up quick, I'm pretty dang sure.

Your health & your freedom is all that you need, even if it's in your "mind" I promise you'll succeed.

The higher the risk, the higher the gain. But what "princi-ples" do you stand on? Are they solid enough to support your frame?

You don't need a yacht, homie, live by your means, but your friend can have one, you know what I mean?

I thought I'd never live past twenty -oh- three. Every day is a blessin, yall remember these things.

Justice Is…

If crime is the opposite of justice,
And crime's mission is [illegible] to all,
then is it logical that justice —
the opposite of crime — is to create
the opposite outcome, that being healing

Justice is not synonymous with punishment,
retribution, or revenge. Rather it is about
[illegible] for hurt people hurt people.
Crime prevention's most effective tool
is compassion and healing that [illegible]
heal the offender [illegible] the [illegible]
Repair the bonds of humanity, for inclusion
acceptance, and belonging [illegible] deterrence.

By [illegible]

JUSTICE IS . . .

JEFFERY L. YOUNG
MCF Stillwater, MN

If crime is the opposite of justice, and crime's outcome is harm to all, then is it logical that justice—the opposite of crime—should create the opposite outcome? That, being healing?

Justice is not synonymous with punishment, retribution, or revenge. Pain is not cured with more pain, for hurt people hurt people. Crime preventor's most effective tool is compassion and healing. Heal the victim, heal the offender, heal the community. Repair the bonds of humanity, for inclusion, acceptance, and belonging repel deviance.

"Tethered"

What I Want to Say to My Heart, How My Heart Responds

By: Toby Earl Johnson

Stand up; you can make it in this life alone. Need of none, be strong!!! Your heart beats on its own, right? Then why need it to carry others? *"But wait—what a fool! What is life without others? If there was all the money to be had, tangibles to retain, would you then be happy? Ha, proved you need someone!"*

But what if it's easier to go without pain, sadness or loss? Are these not good reasons to close ones heart off? *"Well, is there sunshine without rain? Can plants, trees, flowers or even animals grow without water? See, the universe is all contingent on one another as is the human heart to others. Have I convinced you yet?"*

But what happens when it's dark, you feel alone, and you hear your chest beat... where are the others then? *"But what a fool! Did you not talk to loved ones today? Have happy thoughts and memories not come your way? See you heart has been full without even realizing it."*

Ok, so maybe that's true—but if a heart needs a heart, how does a hermit find joy alone on a hill? *"Oh, good question! Does one not think a hermit too did not have a different life? Since infancy, did they raise themselves? Do they still not have the ability to close their eyes and remember loved ones and thoughts of cherished memories? Even today—alone as you'd say, do they not find joy in a creation of splendor, nature, even simple things? See, you can't stand alone. Since birth, every heart has been tethered to someone else, even if but long ago..."*

TETHERED: WHAT I WANT TO SAY TO MY HEART, HOW MY HEART RESPONDS

TOBY EARL JOHNSON
MCF Moose Lake, MN

Stand up; you can make it in this life alone. Need of none, be strong!!! Your heart beats on its own, right? Then why need it carry others? "*But wait—what a fool! What is life without others? If there was all the money to be had, tangibles to retain, would you then be happy? Ha, proved you need someone!*"

But what if it's easier to go without pain, sadness or loss? Are these not good reasons to close ones heart off? "*Well, is there sunshine without rain? Can plants, trees, flowers or even animals grow without water? See, the universe is all contingent on one another as is the human heart to others. Have I convinced you yet?*"

But what happens when it's dark, you feel alone, and you hear your chest beat... where are the others then? "*But what a fool! Did you not talk to loved ones today? Have happy thoughts and memories not come your way? See you heart has been full without even realizing it.*"

Ok, so maybe that's true—but if a heart needs a heart, how does a hermit find joy alone on a hill? "*Oh, good question! Does one not think a hermit too did not have a different life? Since infancy, did they raise themselves? Do they still not have the ability to close their eyes and remember loved ones and thoughts of cherished memories? Even today—alone as you'd say, do they not find joy in a creation of splendor, nature, even simple things? See, you can't stand alone. Since birth, every heart has been tethered to someone else, even if but long ago...*"

"The Ten Weeks of Prison Life" by: Hector [illegible]

"Old hands in the mule business say that the best way to get a stubborn mule's attention is to hit it hard, right between the eyes."

—William Wayne Justice (Senior Federal Judge)

From 1987 till the summer of 1999 I found myself incarcerated in some of the roughest prisons Texas had to offer. In the prison business, when it comes to punishment, Texas reigns supreme on both sides of the fence. For years, I scratched my head wondering why I was able to make it when a lot of "standup" fellas didn't. The answer is I carried myself with honor and respect and I wasn't afraid to pull over an old-timer and ask for some solid advice. That wisdom kept me from being a fresh dummy when I was negotiating prison traffic. It kept me from [illegible], to becoming a wreck.

A "wreck" is southern prison speak for a bad situation or a verbal confrontation that sometimes just comes out of nowhere, even when we try hard to mind our own business. Commonsense wisdom strongly emphasizes to us on a daily basis that we keep our eyes and ears open for shady characters "throwin' bad [illegible]" or "snappin roller skates," again, southern speak for a "wreck."

This is one of many by these, I have [illegible]

THE TEN WRECKS OF PRISON LIFE

HECTOR MEDRANO
Medrano, Rush City, MN

> Old hands in the mule business say that the best way to get a stubborn mules attention is to hit it hard, right between the eyes.
>
> —Willliam Wayne Justice (Iconic federal Judge)

From 1987 till the summer of 1999 I found myself incarcerated in some of the meanest prisons Texas had to offer. In the prison business, when it comes to punishment, Texas reigns supreme, on both sides of the fence. For years, I scratched my head wondering why I was able to make it, when a lot of "stand-up" fellas didn't. The answer is I carried myself with honor and respect and I wasn't afraid to pull over an old firm hand and ask for some solid advice. That wisdom kept me from being a crash dummy when I was negotiating prison traffic. It kept me from causing a "wreck" to becoming a "wreck."

A "wreck" is southern prison speak for a bad situation or a verbal confrontation that sometimes just comes out of nowhere, even when we try hard to mind our own business. Conventional wisdom strongly emphasizes to us on a daily basis that we keep our eyes and ears open for shady characters "throwing banana peels" or "shooting roller skates" again, southern speak for a "wreck".

The point of this article is to try to make your accommodations a little more liveraide. Some of these wrecks I'm still working on, while others are just common sense. We are all still learning "works in progress" just maintain an intense no quit attitude and the results will speak for themselves.

Becoming a fairly decent and respectable inmate or chilly in general has long been a thing of the past. A dying breed on the endangered species list. Like a great song you haven't heard in awhile.

In today's prison system, the majority of the inmate population just want to put their incarceration on "cruise control" until they arrive at their destination which is their projected release date. And if you can avoid "prison traffic" without any

"Tears of a Phoenix"

By Toby Earl Johnson

Is it a sunny day or has hell hailed down upon us?
Windy, smoke blows as if from bellows stoking a fire.
Then, from nowhere, in the purest form of red possible, a phoenix rises
This is not hell, rather the fire of past burdens overcome.

Rebirth, almost as sweet as pure sugarcane.
At times moving fast, others it comes slowly,
Like an earthworm, crawling on dry green sod.
Eyes finally able to see where we've been, mistakes made,
But also focus as clear as a chunk of amber, envisioning a future.

Is this a sunny day or has hell hailed down upon us?
Relief flows inside, no longer having to be the man I once was.
My turquoise tears rolling fervently down my cheeks.
Drip off in rapid succession, almost as if my face is drizzling.

Do I deserve this rebirth the phoenix offers?
Are its tears my healing?
Am I ready for a new chapter in life?
No longer wanting hell, I'm ready for this sunny day!

TEARS OF A PHEONIX

TOBY EARL JOHNSON
MCF Moose Lake, MN

Is it a sunny day or has hell hailed down upon us?
Windy, smoke blows as if from bellows stocking a fire.
Then, from nowhere, in the purest form of red possible, a phoenix rises.
This is not hell, rather the fire of past burdens overcome.

Rebirth, almost as sweet as pure sugarcane.
At times moving fast, others it comes slowly,
Like an earthworm, crawling on dry green sod.
Eyes finally able to see where we've been, mistakes made,
But also focus as clear as a chunk of amber, envisioning a future.

Is this a sunny day or has hell hailed down upon us?
Relief flows inside, no longer having to be the man I once was.
My turquoise tears rolling fervently down my cheeks,
Drip off in rapid succession, almost as if my face is drizzling.

Do I deserve this rebirth the phoenix offers?
Are its tears my healing?
Am I ready for a new chapter in life?
No longer wanting hell, I'm ready for this sunny day!

Bedtime Routine

Fast falls the night, under lock & key,
Peace settles in, no one here but me.
Fans run on high, white noise for sleep.
As sweet as a lullaby, better than counting sheep.
The late news is over, humble prayers are said,
The time has now come, to lay me down to bed.
Thoughts of the past, race through my mind,
Self torture begins, a ritual to unwind.
Oh, Lord, forgive me, the harm that I've done,
Bless those I hurt, and all my loved ones.
Purge my damned soul, free me from sin,
Help me become, human again.
Let me find hope, to face another day,
Soften my heart, please lead the way.
Rid me of demons, who find in me home,
Replace them with angels, from their Heavenly throne
Drape me with dreams, pleasant & sweet,
Let me wake rested, sure on my feet.
Lord, I give thanks, a renewed sense of hope,
Life is still good, in its own proper scope.
My eyes have drawn heavy, weighted & deep,
Thankfully now, I can nod off to sleep.

BEDTIME ROUTINE (POEM)

RYAN N. SORENSEN
Draper Prison, UT

Fast falls the night, under lock and key,
Peace settles in, no one here but me.
Fans run on high, white noise for sleep,
As sweet as a lullaby, better than counting sheep.
The late news is over, humble prayers one said,
The time has now come, to lay me down to bed.
Thoughts of the past, race through my mind,
Self-torture begins, a ritual to unwind.
Oh, Lord, forgive me, the harm that I've done,
Bless those I hurt, and all my loved ones.
Purge my damned soul, free me from sin,
Help me become, human again.
Let me find hope, to face another day,
Soften my heart, please lead the way.
Rid me of demons, who find in me home,
Replace them with angels, from their heavenly throne.
Drape me with dreams, pleasant and sweet,
Let me wake rested, sure on my feet.
Lord, I give thanks, a renewed sense of hope,
Life is still good, in its own proper scope.
My eyes have drawn heavy, weighted and deep,
Thankfully now, I can nod off to sleep.

Time

Can time really heal the pain that I caused,
Or is that something we say to allow a big pause
When we mess up so bad and feel like there's no hope
or when freedom is taken after our choice to use dope.
What can time really do to our brains?
Will we use it wisely, or stay stuck in the game?
I want my son to notice when I'm not around
But does the time spent apart block out the sound
the sound of a mother's affection and love
which is sweeter than angels voices above
Time makes you think about more than the past
You make plans for the future and hope that it lasts
But we remember we're humans and we're scared to fail
Time shows us how much life is truly so frail
You try to be courageous, you try to survive
then you feel guilt and pain, the stress gives you hives
Emotionally broken, alone in this room
Time right now is causing you to feel gloom
Time can be full of remorse and regrets
and thoughts and feelings we've tried to neglect
time is like a rollercoaster there's downs and there's ups
the good thing about time is you learn to be tough
you see how far you've come so you start to smile
You start to see who you are and stop living in denial
We felt lots of pain and weren't afraid to cry
Our life appears to be changing because we are willing to try
You can soon go home to where you belong
It seems that time really did make you strong
Mistakes are forgiven by all of your friends
You are proud of your progress, don't want it to end
So does time really heal all of the pain?
It depends if you use it for personal gain

TIME

SARAH LINDSAY LEWIS
Draper Prison, UT

Can time really heal the pain that I caused, or is that something we say to allow a big pause when we mess up so bad and feel like there's no hope or when freedom is taken after our choice to use dope. What can time really do to our brains? Will we use it wisely, or stay stuck in the game? I want my son to notice when I'm not around. But does the time spent a part block out the sound, the sound of a mother's affection and love which is sweeter than angels voices above. Time makes you think about more than the past. You make plans for the future and hope that it lasts. But we remember we're humans and we're scared to fail. Time shows us how much life is truly so frail. You try to be courageous, you try to survive then you feel guilt and pain, the stress gives you hives. Emotionally broken, alone in this room. Time right now is causing you to feel gloom. Time can be full of remorse and regrets and thoughts and feelings we've tried to neglect. Time is like a rollercoaster there's downs and there's ups. The good thing about time is you learn to be tough. You see how far you've come so you start to smile. You start to see who you are and stop living in denial. We felt lots of pain and weren't afraid to cry. Our life appears to be changing because we are willing to try. You can soon go home to where you belong. It seems that time really did make you strong. Mistakes are forgiven by all of your friends. You are proud of your progress, don't want it to end. So does time really heal all of the pain? It depends if you use it for personal gain. For whatever time that I have left here I choose to be happy and live without fear.

Shatter Visions & Open Heart 10-10-19
By Andrew Esquer

Shatter visions and broken dreams,
life it's not what it seems.
From growing up in a broken home
I shoulda listen and never romed.
Mom and Dad had a change of heart,
and I've been lost from the start.
I grew up fast with no time to play
I still Kept an open heart
to change my way
The pain is real the anger is deep
it hits me hard like a nightmare
when I sleep.
It cuts me deep like a open wound
who Knew the love of my life
would die so soon
when we met
I Knew from the start
it felt like a dream
that open my heart.
Befor she pass we got engaged
Its been 4 Years since that day
Shatter Visions haunt my Past,
but my open heart will forever last,
So hears a Kiss I send to You
my open heart was meat for You.

SHATTER VISION AND OPEN HEART

ANDREW ESQUER
Draper Prison, UT

Shatter visions and broken dreams,
Life it's not what it seems.
From growing up in a broken home
I shoulda listen and never roamed.
Mom and Dad had a change of heart,
And I've been lost from the start.
I grew up fast with no time to play
I still kept an open heart
To change my way
The pain is real the anger is deep
It hits me hard like a nightmare
When I sleep.
It cuts me deep like an open wound
Who knew the love of my life
Would die so soon
When we met
I knew from the start
It felt like a dream
That open my heart.
Before she pass we got engaged.
It's been 4 years since that day
Shatter visions haunt my past,
But my open heart will forever last,
So hears a kiss I send to you
My open heart was meant for you.

Life Love and Pain 11-11-9

By Andrew Esquer

Life love and Pain
Can lead you to the lime light,
or crying in the rain.
Love is from my son
the pain is missing his first words,
or seeing him born.
My life has change from seeing him behind the screen.
It was life love and pain,
but far from a dream
the Pain I can put in many words
its like apart of me died, thats always messing with my mind
his life is bless,
and so is mine
My tears keep running, untill that time.
The day im free, ill show him the way
And tell him my life was empty
untill we met that day
every life takes its turns
it can be for the best
and some we get burned,
but your my world,
and your my son
My pain will be gone
the day I come home.

LIFE LOVE AND PAIN

ANDREW ESQUER
Draper Prison, UT

Life love and pain
Can lead you to the lime light,
Or crying in the rain.
Love is from my son
The pain is missing his first words,
Or seeing him born.
My life has change from seeing him behind the screen.
It was life love and pain,
But far from a dream
The pain I can put in many words
Its like apart of me died, that's always messing with my nerves
His life is bless,
And so is mine
My tears keep running, until that time.
The day I'm free, I'll show him the way.
And tell him my life was empty
Until we met that day
Every life takes its turns
It can be for the best
And some we get burned,
But you're my world,
And you're my son
My pain will be gone
The day I come home.

TIME

So I'm sitting in prison doing some time

For supposedly committing a crazy ol crime

It's sad of the thought of doing years

As I sit here trying to suppress the tears

How can 5 people make so many choices?

About our lives with out their voices

They decide our fate in a hidden room

Then drop the bomb and it seals our doom

It started with a Judge dropping the mallet

Then they shove us in cells like stacking a pallet

How long I'll sit here only God can tell

In this lame ol place of a man made hell

There's so much hatred and discontent

I wonder where every ones kindness went

TIME

RUSTY CLARK
Draper Prison, UT

So I'm sitting in prison doing some time
For supposedly committing a crazy ol crime
It's sad of the thought of doing years
As I sit here trying to suppress the tears
How can 5 people make so many choices?
About our lives without their voices
They decide our fate in a hidden room
Then drop the bomb and it seals our doom
It started with a judge dropping the mallet
Then they shove us in cells like stacking a pallet
How long I'll sit here only God can tell
In this lame ol place of a man made hell
There's so much hatred and discontent
I wonder where everyone's kindness went
I can hear people sharpening shanks
I know that they're not just playing pranks
In this place you get stabbed with steel
The deep down wounds will never heal
People have more stories than Dr. Seuss
So many lies, it leaves me confused
They lock us in cells like caged up beast
And feed us slop in non-fulfilling feasts
They look through our windows like counting sheep
They count us all night as we sleep
We close our eyes to many different dreams
And adventure the times with various themes
In this cell there's a toilet and sink
The leave you there so you can think
Think about things and what you would change
Think of the past How it was deranged
Can't fix the past, only change the future
Only mend the past like using a suture

Sometimes it won't heal and leaves a scar
That's just a reminder how bad times are
So here I am wasting my short life span
Sitting here decaying in PrisneyLand

Karma Instigated war exposing secrets and fears.
Always playing games just to see some tears.
Through out the years she's got good at war.
Taking our riches making us poor.
The retribution she seeks words can't explain.
Tearing families apart, leaving hearts in pain.
[illegible] many deep scars causing unbearable stress.
All the hate a [illegible]
They say the war isn't [illegible] till the storm has p[illegible]sed
And [illegible] it is over only the str[illegible] will last.
The strong will continue to fight the war again.
Until that hateful day may [illegible] the end.

Rusty 191830

KARMA

RUSTY CLARK
Draper Prison, UT

Karma's initiated war exposing secrets and fears.
Always playing havoc just to see some tears.
Throughout the years the years she's got good at war.
Taking our riches, making us poor.
The retribution she seeks, words can't explain.
Tearing families apart, leaving hearts in pain.
So many deep scars causing unbearable stress.
All the hate and hurt leaves our lives a mess.
They say the war isn't over till the storm has passed.
And once it is over only the strong will last.
The strong will continue to fight the war again.
Until that hateful day may your life you mend.

It's crazy when I stop and see
The person I've become to be
I've lost my faith in myself and so
I need to find me so I can grow
I've always known who had my back
It's strange to me, this confidence I now lack
The best one to have my back was me
So who is this stranger that now I see
I trusted the ones who didn't care
Turned my back on the ones that were always there
Hate and anger have found their place
The holes in my faith, they've filled that space
At the end of the day it's only me
Standing nude in the mirror, the truth to see
Where once I was always proud of all said and done
Now I'm disappointed that I was the one
When did I turn my back on all that was me
When just like the rest did I start to be

DEAR ME

CHERIE CLARK
Draper Prison, UT

It's crazy when I stop and see
The person I've become to be
I've lost my faith in myself and so I need to find me so I can grow
I've always known who had my back
It's strange to me, this confidence I not lack
The best one to have my back was me
So who is this stranger that now I see
I trusted the ones who didn't care
Turned my back on the ones that were always there
Hate and anger have found their place
The holes in my faith, they've filled that space
At the end of the day it's only me
Standing nude in the mirror, the truth to see
Where once I was always proud of all said and done
Now I'm disappointed that I was the one
When did I turn my back on all that was me
When just like the rest did I start to be
What will it take to get back to my pride
And put all this disappointment aside
and Am I too late to fix from within
Do I have the courage it takes to begin
Wtho will I welcome as the new me reveals
Who will be waiting to try turning my wheels
All of these questions are all very good
Now it's up to me to get back as I should
If I don't come back from this life I call mine
Then you'll know where to find me, I'll be doing time
How you lost all control with the smoke and the wine

Do you have what is needed to come back to me
To stand alone if that's what's to be
I know that it's in you,
I know that you can
        I know that there's no way I can stay as I am
        I have all the faith and I need you to see
        You have all that is needed, You have Me.

Tell Me Dear God
By Mauree L. Graham

Tell me dear god
Did you die__ like they said
Or are you trapped behind bars
Getting' high__ like your kids,

Condemned wit' no peace
Feeling the pain of frustration
Tryin' to bear with your grief
So traumatized _ you're shakin'

Do your daydreams lie
Like mine__ at the grave
Have you found that in life
Getting' by__ is escape

I know your story is hard – oh so hard
So please tell me dear god – yes my god!

Prison Mother
By Mauree L. Graham

There's a lovely face

TELL ME DEAR GOD

MAURECE L. GRAHAM
Faribault Prison, MN

Tell me dear god
Did you die_ like they said
Or are you trapped behind bars
Gettin' high_ like your kids,

Condemned wit' no peace
Feeling the pain_ of frustration
Tryin' to bear with your grief
So traumatized_ you're shakin'

Do your daydreams lie
Like mine_ at the grave
Have you found that in life
Gettin' by_ is escape.

I know your story is hard—oh so hard
So please tell me dear god—yes my god!

LUV

By Maurece L. Graham

I think of Luv
Like a butterfly
A beautiful delight
That colors our lives

I picture Luv
Like a waterspring
Shaping destiny
in its impromptu streams

I contemplate Luw

LUV

MAURECE L. GRAHAM
Faribault Prison, MN

I think of Luv
Like a butterfly
A beautiful delight
That colors our lives

I picture Luv
Like a waterspring
Shaping destiny
In its impromptu streams

I contemplate Luv
As a peregrine
Soaring intensely
Impervious to chagrin

I see Luv
As a smiling face
A tender reminder
Of why I have faith

And I know of Luv
As what we have
The togetherness that molds us
From the unforgettableness of our past

To my Baby Brother, Jackie Luv Graham

WHAT ABOUT THE NEIGHBORS??
By Maurece L. Graham

It is listen-to-the-teapot-simmer quiet,
And as the susurrus sounds of
boiling herb reach you,
So does the bitter-tainted
smell of limp, wet leaves,
Both awaiting a dollop of honey,
which you add – as you pour –
And you hear "plop"
because it is *that* quiet,
The tingling din of your spoon
tapping and dinging against
Your porcelain mug as you mix,
chasing away the
Subtler sounds of the dark,
matriculating liquid
which you bring lover-like
to your lips,
Replacing silence
with the almost
raucous crash of a perfect slurp
the silence is so cloying you

WHAT ABOUT THE NEIGHBORS

MAURECE L. GRAHAM
Faribault Prison, MN

It is listen-to the-teapot-simmer quiet,
And as the susurrus sounds of
   boiling herb reach you,
So does the bitter-tainted
   smell of limp, wet leaves,
Both awaiting a dollop of honey,
   which you add—as you pour—
And you hear "plop"
   because it is *that* quiet,
The tingling ding of your spoon
   tapping and dinging against
Your porcelain mug as you mix,
   chasing away the
Subtler sounds of the dark,
   matriculating liquid
Which you bring lover-like
   to your lips,
Replacing silence
   with the almost
Raucous crash of a perfect slurp
   the silence is so cloying you
Prepare to shout—
   and then a thought occurs to you:
What about the neighbors?

PRISON MOTHER

MAURECE L. GRAHAM
Faribault Prison, MN

There's a lovely face
Inside my mind
What a lovely face

You should see the eyes
You should see the hair
Should see the smile
Should see just what makes
Me feel so proud
If I were in a crowd
I'd turn around
Give a knowing smile
And take a bow
Won't help but notice
The gleam in my eyes
Cause my joy inside
Never burned so bright

All around I see
The perfection of love
And what it means to me
Is the essence of "us"
And equally
I miss your hugs
What a healing grace
To feel your touch

If nature and family
Uplift and uphold
Then creation
Is your mold
Counterbalance to a world

That can feel so cold
Restored balance to a world
In need of some hope

Life's been a chance
(And yes, I've suffered)
But how else could your light
Have reached the minds of others
I've adored this chance
I'll spread it one to another
Let 'em catch a glimpse…

Of a Truly Wonderful Mother!

You Know Him.

You Know Him.
Or At Least You...
His Family Seemed Nice Enough,
He Wasn't An [illegible] ...
Went To The Same School,
Though He Lived Across The Bridge.
Sure, It's Different Where He's Living,
Not That The Choice Was His...
But

You Know Him.
At Least You Think You Do
I Mean, You Recently Talked
But When You Did, Well, It Was Cool.
So, When You Think Of Him Though,
Of Course You Get Confused.
Cause, If You Know Him Like You Think You Do,
How Come "He" [illegible] You.

Truth Is: "He" Could Be Anyone
And That Just Goes To Show
It Wasn't What You Thought You Knew,
But, What You Didn't Know...

Do You Know Him...

La Guerre
Oct. 18th 2014

YOU KNOW HIM

GAETHAN LAGUERRE
Draper Prison, UT

You know him.
Or at least you thought you did.
His family seemed nice enough,
He wasn't an awful kid.
He went to the same school,
Though he lived across the bridge.
Sure, it's different where he's living,
Not that the choice was his...
But

You know him.
Or at least you think you do.
I mean, you rarely talked
But when you did, well, it was cool.
So, when you think of him today,
Of course you get confused.
'Cause, if you know him like you think you do,
How come "he" isn't you?

Truth is! "He" could be anyone
And that just goes to show
It wasn't what you thought you knew,
But, what you didn't know...

Do you know him?

[illegible]

[illegible]

[illegible] First Day of [illegible]

[illegible]

[illegible]

[illegible]

KEYON WUZ HERE

GAETHAN LAGUERRE
Draper Prison, UT

Keyon Jr. is starting his first day of high school. This is the time in his life when he is supposed to be finding himself. He walks into his homeroom and sits in the back. His teacher begins to read off the names on the roll and pauses as she reads his: "Keyon . . . Harris?" There was a tinge of recognition in her voice, as if she'd known that name for years. She and Keyon lock eyes and she asks, "Are you Keyon Harris' son, the one from the south end?" He thinks for a while and shakes his head, "No."

The teacher does not respond, instead she proceeds as if the exchange never happened. Keyon can see through her though, she's afraid.

He leans back in his chair, lulled by the rhythm of the chalk hitting the board. He looks down at a desk, much like all of the ones he's sat in in middle school, and sees something familiar yet altogether new to him . . . "Keyon wuz here."

MY HAND

SEAN SWAIN
Ohio Department of Rehabilitation and Correction, OH

This is my hand,
With this hand pressed to the fiberglass I greet those who come to visit.
This hand gripped ten thousand captive nights.
This hand chased friends from the maelstorm of teargas and blood.
This hand, My hand.
This hand fights for liberation
Yours and mine
Because so long as one of us is chained
None of us are free.
This hand sharpened pencil stubs on a concrete floor
wrote a history of oppression to outlive oppressors.
This hand will one day shade my eyes from the brilliant light of the sun,
Brush fragile blades of grass,
Caress the ocean's rolling cold,
Hold my newborn child.
This hand will one day form a clenched fist of victory
Over those who build fences.
With this hand pressed to the fiberglass I smuggle to you the only gift I can afford,
Past unsuspecting guards
Who cannot fathom the true danger of a one-word message...
FREEDOM.

I SHALL NOT DIE

SEAN SWAIN
Ohio Department of Rehabilitation and Correction, OH

I shall not die
A thousand deaths of compromise
Giving up names in exchange
For food or a blanket.
I will bite my own arm
To smother my screams
And rob you of satisfaction
When you disassemble me.

I shall not dies
Shamefully, my chin to my chest kneeling before the humiliating hole
I dug for myself,
Waiting upon the pistol shot.
I will always refuse the blindfold.

I shall not die
Abandoned and alone
Obliterated from the memories
of those I love,
My date never questioned.
Someone will always stand in the rain

Outside your office window,
My name on a cardboard sign.
I shall not die.
A thousand time—
I shall not die.
You will only get my corpse.

UNFINISHED SONG

SEAN SWAIN
Ohio Department of Rehabilitation and Correction, OH

If you do not kill me now
RIGHT NOW
I will become an ANTHEM
That your ENEMIES will sing
When they RESIST you.
But if you kill me now
RIGHT NOW
I will forever remain
The UNFINISHED SONG
That your CHILDREN will compose
Again and again
Until they DEFEAT you.

WRETCHED OF THE EARTH

SEAN SWAIN
Ohio Department of Rehabilitation and Correction, OH

I was born in freedoms graveyard 'neath a tombstone
where my name scarred the edifice, stone cold and bare
hand, wrapped was I in burning flag.
An empty stomach, angry, held tight another fist to
cleetch the long night
Another head fixed 'twixt the gun sight—
Just one more toe to tag.

Raised by ashes in dirt and dust cutting teeth then flesh
on rust they come to teach me what is just—
The oppressors' fists to kiss me.

So when I taste that awful wrath kicked down that darkly—
chosen path I'll see it boils down to math—
How many I take with me.

FUGITIVE THOUGHTS

SEAN SWAIN
Ohio Department of Rehabilitation and Correction, OH

The distant tree line beyond the yard stirs yearnings too intense.
My thoughts often escape me
And take a blind run for the fence.

Sometimes the tower shoots them
Sometimes the dogs attack
They're always butchered bloody
By the time I get them back.

Sometimes they're dead and dangling
Sometimes they get away
Just to find no place to go
But that's the price they pay.

You too may see this window's view
Or face the gallows pole
So if you harbor my fugitive thoughts
Don't ever tell a soul.

RESPONSE TO ODRC COUNSEL TREVOR MATTHEW CLARK'S LECTURE ON ADVOCATING POLITICAL VIOLENCE

SEAN SWAIN
Ohio Department of Rehabilitation and Correction, OH

Denunciations fall lifeless,
Corpses tumbling from a mass grave
Your mouth
Twenty-three years of boot heels
Persuading the back of my neck
Your waggling finger
A conquistadors sword
Your hand gripping tender ankles
My unborn
Dashing their heads upon the altar
Your desk
Where the blood of ancestors seeps
From a leather briefcase
And I think if I could shake these chains
(and cuffs and shackles)
For just a few seconds
I could prove to you
And to all the unavenged ghosts in the room
How so incredibly fiercely I share
The states intentions of peace.

The Jour Home
Before drug addi g
Before g and Staying up late
I had a perception of drug add
After spending time in jail and prison I know that I'm s
I am sure after years upon years I was wrong
After picking up that pipe and smoking the bong
I grew up with a very white priveleged life
Getting everything I wanted and living without strife
I had it all husband, house, son, car, dog
But no one knew my head was in a fog
I was rejected and broken and had no self love
I had no belief system in anything above
I taught high school kids who were at high risk
of ending up in places very similar to this
I ended up committing a sexual crime
without thinking how it would affect my time
The time that I needed to spend with my son
being a mom and having so much fun
When I was first booked into Utah County Jail
everything about my life was an epic fail
I met women who had been through it all
Drugs, rape, neglect is what led them to fall
I listened to their stories and most made me cry
I thought back on my life and then wondered why
why did I judge other humans like this
They are the strongest and bravest and have true g
I gained great respect for these women so dear
as I sat in the jail for almost a year
I was introduced to meth while sitting in a cell
I snorted my first line which would later become
I was released from jail with no money and nohom
and once again I was feeling alone
I contacted a girl I was in jail with

THE JOURNEY HOME

SARAH LINDSAY LEWIS
Draper Prison, UT

Before I was a drug addict at the age of 28
Before I was tweaking and staying up late
I had a perception of what drug addicts were
After spending time in jail and prison I know that I'm sure
I am sure after years up years I was wrong
After picking up that pipe and smoking the bong
I grew up with a very while privileged life
Getting everything I wanted and living without strife
I had it all husband, house, son, car, dog
But no one knew my head was in a fog
I was rejected and broken and had no self love
I had no belief system in anything above
I taught high school kids who were at high risk
Of ending up in places very similar to this
I ended up committing a sexual crime
Without thinking how it would affect my time
The time that I needed to spend with my son
Being a mom and having so much fun
When I was first booked into Utah County Jail
Everything about my life was an epic fail
I met women who had been through it all
Drugs, rape, neglect is what led them to fall
I listened to their stories and most made me cry
I thought back on my life and then wondered why
Why did I judge other humans like this
They are the strongest and bravest and have true grit
I gained great respect for these women so dear
As I sat in jail for almost a year
I was introduced to meth while sitting in a cell
I snorted my first line which would later become hell
I was released from jail with no money and no home
And once again I was feeling alone

I contacted a girl I was in jail with
She became my best friend, my dealer, my personal gift
I tried every drug I could get my hands on
Mostly to numb the loss of custody of my son
Using drugs alone was simply not enough
I wanted to hustle I wanted to be tough
I started to make my way up the chain
While working with suppliers of various gangs
I thought I had a better way to sell drugs
I even avoided the use of big thugs
I then got too cocky with all that I knew
And got snitched out by a girl so brand new
The judge sent me to prison in a heartbeat
It happened so fast he did not even blink
I am thankful that I got caught when I did
Because I still have a chance at a life with my kid.

The Whispers

Whisper
Wayward Words Rest
On
Tears With Tenderness'
The Heart Hates
The Mind Knows
But Lives
With The Whisper.

Silence Is Loud
Filled With Emptiness
Fear Is Comfort

Nothing, Perfect
Something, Is Ruined
Abundant

THE WHISPERS

GAETHAN LAGUERRE
Draper Prison, UT

Whispers.
Wretched words rest
On treacherous tongues.
Tense with transgressions
The heart hates
The mind knows
But the soul lives
With the whispers.
Silence is loud
Filled with emptiness
Crowded by loneliness
Fear is comfort
Death is certain
Nothing, is perfect
Something, is flawed
Abundant
With the whispers

How Blessed

In prison guys talk about their kids with equal amount of pride and shame. Then they ask about mine.

She told me about the baby in a bodega across the street from my first apartment. I froze in the aisle. She walked casually. I stared at generic popcorn exposed through a clear plastic slot—how fast the kernel explodes, changing all but its purpose to be consumed. The expression on my face must have stilled the speech she prepared. She came back, looked at me like we'd done this before, sighed and moved to the next aisle.

At the register I paid for our small items. I felt the scorn of the Pakistani clerk because this wasn't the same woman I'd typically accompany— I grabbed some batteries I didn't need off a little rack and asked for a pack of Swisher Sweet cigarillos in the cellophane of my sullen bubble without eye contact.

But it wasn't my place to pay for what she'd decided.

Her grief gone, bundled in a red bio-hazard bag with the small moments of the clinic: how the two women waiting didn't speak, the article she half read then forgot, the iron thud of blood and chemical like cell bars slamming. We still spent the night together—my lust, an explosion of helpless negotiation. This vapid passion, the only way I knew to say good-bye.

Had she told me, I would have fought,
I would've fashioned a new world—so I tell myself.

That bag of popcorn from the bodega sat on the bench seat of my truck for days, the batteries on the dash soaking in the sun to explode. The woman I'd been living with opened the popcorn without asking and I looked at her like she had murdered my unborn child. All I saw was the other woman; a hollow space released once the plastic tore, my child's mind reeling into adult prices as I am reminded—

This ain't no place for children

C. Fausto Cabrera

HOW BLESSED

C. FAUSTO CABRERA
Rush City Prison, MN

In prison guys talk about their kids with equal amount of pride and shame. Then they ask about mine.

She told me about the baby in the bodega across the street from my first apartment. I froze in the aisle. She walked casually. I stared at generic popcorn exposed through a clear plastic slot—how fast the kernel explodes, changing all but its purpose to be consumed. The expression on my face must have stifled the speech she prepared. She came back, looked at me like we'd done this before, sighed and moved to the next aisle.

At the register I paid for small items. I felt the scorn of the Pakistani clerk because this wasn't the same woman I'd typically accompany—I grabbed some batteries I didn't need off a little rack and asked for a pack of Swisher Sweet cigarillos in the cellophane of my sullen bubble without eye contact.

But it wasn't my place to pay for what she'd decided.

Her grief gone, bundled in a red biohazard bag with the small moments of the clinic: how the two women waiting didn't speak, the article she half read then forgot, the iron thud of blood and chemical like cell bars slamming. We still spent the night together—my lust, an expulsion of helpless negotiation. This vapid passion, the only way I knew to say good-bye.

Had she told me, I would have fought,

I would've fashioned a new world—so I tell myself.

That bag of popcorn from the bodega sat on the bench seat of my truck for days, the batteries on the dash soaking in the sun to explode. The woman I'd been living with opened the popcorn without asking and I looked at her like *she* had murdered my unborn child. All I saw was the other woman; a hollow space released once the plastic tore, my child's mind reeling into adult prices as I am reminded—

This ain't no place for children.

When I Asked Him What He Was Reading

"I've read five books in my life," he said.
He may have been dyslexic, Lord knows
juvenile incarceration wouldn't have caught it.

"Three of them in segregation."
His second stretch in ten years, he bought
a TV the first week; only watched
when the cage closed, dozing
Nick @ Nite to *Archie Bunker*—
hearing the ol' man snicker and sleep.

"A romance without sex scenes, a western
with a fake-ass cowboy sheriff,"
his rapid chuckle, a linebacker build.
My cell boxed down by books,
creepy crawled on his skin
as he shifted.

"And one about a guy getting breaks.
Like me, he'd cry to his family, to God—
whoever'd answer.
He'd bend them till he broke."
He picked up a paperback dictionary

leafing through the corners like a flipbook

hoping to see a stick figure run. Then

slapped it in his vast palm.

"I thought stories were supposed to end happy, ya know?
Otherwise what's the point?
Anyway,
I tore out the last chapter
so it couldn't hurt anyone else in the dark."

© Fausto Cabrera

WHEN I ASKED HIM WHAT HE WAS READING

C. FAUSTO CABRERA
Rush City Prison, MN

"I've read five books in my life," he said.
He may have been dyslexic, Lord
knows
Juvenile Incarceration wouldn't have
caught it.

"Three of them in segregation."
His second stretch in ten years, he
bought
a TV the first week; only watched
when the cage closed, dozing
Nick @ Nite to Archie Bunker—
hearing the ol' man snicker and slurp.

"A romance without sex scenes, a western
with a fake-ass cowboy sheriff,"
his rapid chuckle, a linebacker build.
My cell bared down by books,
creepy crawled on his skin
as he shifted.

"And one about a guy getting breaks.
Like me, he'd cry to his family, to God—
whoever'd answer.
He'd bend them till be broke."
He picked up a paperback dictionary
leafing through the corners like a flipbook
hoping to see a stick figure run.
Then Slapped it in his vast palm.

"I thought stories were supposed to end happy, ya know?
Otherwise what's the point?
Anyway,
I tore out the last chapter
so it couldn't hurt anyone else in the dark."

A Ladybug's Visit

Found in the thick of a cell,
without branch or brush,
where no green grows,
I sit caged, waiting
to box the world.

She need not say a word
through the wonder of being,
an accidental spark, with brightened
brick shell. I watched, waited, for her
to flee to flashing bulbs of all florescent
as I sat in the shadow of a two-way mirror

The lore says, make a wish and let her fly,
but what was the point, a written prayer
                                        creased on paper plane.

She could've flown anywhere,
at any time, but she stayed
leaving indelible marks—
a weightlessness of touch
She wouldn't crawl onto my finger,

A LADYBUG'S VISIT

C. FAUSTO CABRERA
Rush City Prison, MN

Found in the thick of a cell,
without branch or brush,
where no green grows,
I sit caged, waiting
to box the world.

She need not say a word
Through the wonder of being,
An accidental spark, with brightened
brick shell. I watched, waited, for her
to flee to flashing bulbs of all fluorescent
As I sat in the shadow of a two-way mirror

The lore says, make a wish and let her fly,
But what was the point, a written prayer
creased on paper plane.

She could've flown anywhere,
At any time, but she stayed
leaving indelible marks—
A weightlessness of touch.
She wouldn't crawl onto my finger,

But she didn't leave my side, lingering in the silhouette
Of my glass reflection.
In her shined smile
I appeared polished.

Could I know her heart like I believe
God knows mine? If so how
could I translate the unspoken, decoding
Whispers of another life through
truth of need and lies of want
Or need of lies as I want of truth.

And then, like everything, she was gone

Pill (tific Killers)

Solar flares ignite the
Auroras b sky bright
Pin prick souls falling into flame
Warming globe who is to blame?

I've shorn my head to break the habit
worrying rats de a maze
crust is thin we dine upon
The is cracked and spidered now

W ust feed them to survive the breakage
Repair the mast before the storm
The chocking child is he breathing
From dark to light a babe is born

Strike match and scar the sadness
Cauterize the weeping wound
Calender and clock t ing backwards
Golden sun and silver moon

Tell me now what does it mean?
Tell me now what do you feel?
Doctor ~~Doctor please~~ I ~~feed~~ the pill
To calm my ache to cure my ill

S tific Killers f kind
Scientific Killers of mankind

THE PILL (SCIENTIFIC KILLERS)

JACOB BURROW
Draper Prison, UT

Solar tares ignite the fabric
Auroras burning bright
Pin prick souls falling into flame
Warming globe who is to blame?

I've shorn my head to break the habit
Scurrying rats inside a maze
The crust is thin we dine upon
The ice is cracked and spidered now

We must feed them to survive the breakage
Repair the mast before the storm
The choking child is he breathing
From dark to light a babe is born

Strike the match and scar the sadness
Cauterize the weeping wound
Calendar and clock are turning backwards
Golden sun and silver moon

Tell me now what does it mean?
Tell me now what do you feel?
Doctor, Doctor please I need the pill
To cure my ache To cure my ill

Scientific killers of mankind
Scientific killers of mankind.

HOPE FROM THE BACK OF THE CLOSET

RYAN N. SORENSEN
Draper Prison, UT

Can someone please make sense of the systematic warehousing of society's undesirables? What is the message we portray for the world to see as we stow away human lives like clothing we shove to the back of the closet never to be used again? Who has the vision to seek out those disregarded lives and to repurpose them with hope and renewed faith in humanity? Who has the time to spend on a lost cause?

Humanity has a way of salvaging the dregs of society through our inherent will to survive. Take everything away from me & I will learn to appreciate the most simple acts of kindness. A smile or kind word becomes more valuable than anything money can buy. Family & friends are not taken for granted, rather are cherished for the hope & strength they provide us.

Regrets? There will always be regrets, but regret begets compassion. Suddenly, its not about "me" & my needs. "You" become the focus of our energy. How can I help you?

Humanity is restored when we believe in the amazing resiliency of a man's soul and allows regret & pain to become stepping stones towards inner peace & civility. This is when true freedom becomes reality and a disregarded life can be nurtured & strengthened despite being shoved to the back of the closet.

Duhe

An allegory by C.H. Williams

Rigid regimentation is a defining feature of prison life. Unseen by the good, law-abiding folk outside in the free world, the forced habituation of life behind bars can take many forms, and does, yet it is always a systematic top-down process of dominance and control played out and reinforced in countless mini dramas every day, all designed to teach the inmate his place. Essentially, to make him heel. The goal is that [illegible] teach the [illegible] good behavior through classic conditioning techniques – extreme forms of punishment blended with sparse positive reinforcement – it stands to reason the convict may take this learned behavior to the real world once released, thereby becoming a productive, law-abiding citizen. And some do. But the end result too often backfires, leaving its mark on the prisoner long after release and coming back to bite the law-abiding citizenry right in the ass. In fact, recidivism figures show that this regimentation process, as perfected by the California Department of Corrections and Rehabilitation over the past three decades, rarely works as designed.

Imagine, every moment of every day follows a schedule, from the minute cell doors are unlocked in the morning to the instant they are spike-locked at night. At many of the state's prisons, the daily schedule is punctuated by the sound of a bell. I'm not talking the slow dong of an old time church bell, or the ding ding a-ling of a come-and-get-it dinner bell. No. I'm talking high-pitched, long-sustained, state-of-the-art in digital electronics, deafening loud and insufferably annoying got-your-attention-now-boy? Prison bell. The kind you hear for a few uncertain seconds after the actual blast has stopped.

At Soledad's Correctional Training Facility, for instance, the bell shakes prisoners out of bed promptly at 5:30 a.m. Its ring herds them to breakfast at six, drives them along to their job and school assignments sharply at eight, and later breaks everyone for lunch. The bell gives notice to resume work, then ushers the lot back to their cells when the work-day is done. Two blasts stands-up the entire prison population to be

DUKE: AN ALLEGORY

C.H. WILLIAMS
Draper Prison, UT

Rigid regimentation is a defining feature of prison life. Unseen by the good, law-abiding folk outside in the free world, the forced habituation of life behind bars can take many forms, and does, yet it is always a systematic top-down process of dominance and control played out and reinforced in countless mini dramas every day, all designed to teach the inmate his place. Essentially, to make him heel. The goal is ideal enough: teach the felon good behavior through classical conditioning techniques—extreme forms of punishments blended with sparse positive reinforcement—it stands to reason the convict *may* take this learned behavior to the real world once released, thereby becoming a productive, law-abiding citizen. And some do. But the end result too often backfires, leaving its mark on the prisoner long after release and coming back to bite the law-abiding citizenry right in the ass. In fact, recidivism figures show that this regimentation process, as perfected by the California Department of Corrections and Rehabilitation over the past three decades, rarely works as designed.

Imagine, every moment of every day follows a schedule, from the minute cell doors are unlocked in the morning to the instant they are spike-locked at night. At many of the state's prisons, the daily schedule is punctuated by the sound of a bell. I'm not talking the slow dong of an old church bell, or the ding ding a-ling of a come-and-get-it dinner bell. No. I'm talking high-pitched, long-sustained, state-of-the-art in digital electronics, deafening loud and insufferably annoying got-your-attention-now-boy? Prison bell. The kind you hear for a few uncertain seconds after the actual blast has stopped.

At Soledad's Correctional Training Facility, for instance, the bell shakes prisoners out of bed promptly at 5:30 a.m. Its ring herds them to breakfast at six, drives them along to their job and school assignments sharply at eight, and later breaks everyone for lunch. The bell gives notice to resume work, hen ushers the lot back to their cells when the work-day is done. Two blasts stands-up the entire prison population to be counted, three for an emergency count. The bell finally gives one long blast at 9:45 p.m., signifying final lock-up. As a rule—and it is a rule—prisoners do not move without the bells permission.

Guards and other prison personnel rely on the bell, too. The orderly operation of the prison is often disrupted by a string of short continuous bursts, sounds the alarm whenever a fight breaks out between two inmates, rushing all the guards in the world to the scene where they dive *en masse* on top of the two combatants, separate, handcuff, then further restrain them by applying the obligatory headlocks, kidney punches, groin kicks, eye gouges, hairpulls, and a variety of complicated arm twisting and bending techniques which are top secret and taught under a strict code of silence at California's famed prison guard training academy.

"Bells, bells, bells..." wrote Edgar Allen Poe, and prisoners can relate. You hear these bells so many times a day at Soledad, after a while you hardly hear them at all. And like the Eloi of H.G. Wells's *Time Machine*, the principle of conditioning occurs with time and the interminable repetitive sounds of the bells, eventually training a group of people to respond to the sound in a way that becomes habitual, subconscious, even self-defeating.

Standing at the cell door one day, anticipating the lunch bell, my cellie Duke drew a comparison between the prison's bell and Pavlov's. I asked why he had to stand at the door, why he couldn't just kick back and relax while waiting for his grub. He turned his head toward me and he smiled mischievously under his watchcap. "We're Pavlov's dogs, cellie, Pavlov's dogs."

I didn't really get it at first, wasn't yet familiar with Psych 101, but when the bell announcing lunch finally sounded, Duke barked loudly. When our door popped open he smiled at me, barked again, then broke for the chow line.

I laughed to myself. His parody was more accurate than I cared to admit. It was fascinating to consider just how much my 21st Century prison cell resembled a 19th Century Russian kennel.

The truth of his observation wasn't lost on Duke either. As a lark, or maybe just to hear the homeys laugh down the tier, he began barking by the door every time he heard the bell. *Every* time! Usually he waited expectantly by the door, panting occasionally to emphasize the moment, the excitement of anticipation. But funniest of all, when a bell rang off in the distance, as in another cell block, he would whine and yip and growl as if he were being teased.

It was clever and good imitation. If he had a tail I'm sure it would have been wagging. I found myself darting up at the breakfast bell, not because of the annoying bell but because I was afraid Duke would start licking my face.

Despite the absurdity, even something that funny can get old in a hurry, like any joke repeatedly told. It wasn't long before I began ignoring him when he barked, hoping to not encourage him. Unfortunately, as any dog owner will attest, this approach only prompted him to bark with more urgency. Nothing worked. I even tried striking up a conversation when I knew the bell was about to ring, only to be shouted down at the first piercing sound.

Soon I called him on it, explaining that it just wasn't funny anymore. I told him that having a cellie who only spoke German Shepherd was irritating and, worse, the neighbors were starting to talk. I contemplated pooling his homeys to do an intervention—Soledad style. That could get outa hand fast enough, though, as there isn't a convict alive without some form of boundary issues. In the end all I could do was threaten to purchase a muzzle through a mail-order dog obedience agency.

He said he understood and agreed to abandon his canine ways. But we quickly learned his behavior was habitual. He was conditioned and really couldn't help himself. Whenever the bell rang, Duke responded like and eager Beagle. He would catch himself almost at once, a forlorn look of misery creeping across his face. To this day it is difficult for my old cellie to refrain from doing his dog thing when he hears a bell, although regular sessions with the prison shrink are helping.

About a hundred miles up 101, normal operations at San Quentin ran similarly, but the bell there sound more like a foghorn. SQ prisoners, traditionally lifers and long-termers, have a long and storied history of finding and serving most of the speaker wires—if not disabling the public address system altogether. They do not need a foghorn to tell them the morning's mush is already cold.

The bell system symbolizes a way of life for California prisoners, and most of the time it serves it function faithfully. How would prisons operate in an orderly manner without it? More to the point, how do ex-convicts function in society without it?

With 5% of the world's population, the United States holds 25% of the world's prisoners. And California operates the largest prison bureaucracy in the country. Many of its three dozen prisons, recently home to as many as 170,000 inmates (the US Supreme Court recently ordered the state to reduce this number by 30,000... even with the most trained, highest paid guards in the world, California's prisons were not operating in a safe and secure manner.) of every creed and shade, rely on the bell system.

The long-term effects of this conditioning are now predictable, supported by volumes of statistics: the prison shrink is certain that when Duke is unleashed on society he will bite somebody.

LIFE IS All DAY I cant why? Hope WithOUT Faith, LONEly lOST, AlWAYS AFRIad, Life Is all DAY... It IS up TO ME FOR MY DReams TO COME TRUE,.. WITH OUT HOPE NOTHING CAN COME TOO. Always AFRIad, LIFE IS all DAY. TIME COMES and IT goes.. IN THIS TIME Hope SHOULD grow, but NO Faith SO Hope IS NOWHERE TO HOLD.. LIFE IS All Day.. TRY TO TRUST SO Faith CAN HOPE AND NO LONGER will I NEED TO BE afRIad. TO Hope IN my life THAT IS All Day...

VICTOR Pando.

a pome I wrote from my cell IN Imperial County Jail AD Seg. a me to share with you I AM all For SAVING THE kids I would like more INFO on how TO help my relase date Is 9/16/19 So any INFO please SEND TO 422 W NINTH ST my home address.

Pando

HOPE IN LIFE

VICTOR PANDO
Draper Prison, UT

Life is all day.
I can't why?
Hope without faith, lonely lost, always afraid.
Life is all day. . .
It is up to me for my dreams to come true ..
Without hope nothing can come too.
Always afraid, life is all day.
Time comes and it goes . . .
In this time hope should grow,
but no faith so hope is nowhere to hold . . .
Life is all day. . .
Try to trust so faith can home and no longer will I need to be afraid.
To hope in my life that is all day . . .

EDITORIAL BOARD

MARISOL ADRIANA BURGUEÑO
Editor
m.a.burgueno@gmail.com

Marisol Adriana Burgueño has dedicated her career to public advocacy and to the intersections of design and social impacts. Marisol received her MA in Product Design & Development from ELISAVA Barcelona School of Engineering and holds a BA in Industrial Design from the California College of the Arts. Marisol began her career through various roles in product design and visual communications for social entrepreneurship companies. After leaving the for-profit sector she mobilized her knowledge of design and her background in communications to work with nonprofit anti-violence organizations and educational programs for underserved youth in the Bay Area. Marisol's goals are fueled by her passion for ending the cycles of violence and poverty in her community, and building an equitable, interconnected society. She is committed to strengthening community partnerships, increasing access to resources, and public awareness.

DR. ANTHONY J. NOCELLA II
Editor
nocellat@yahoo.com

Anthony J. Nocella II, PhD is an associate professor of criminology and criminal justice at Salt Lake Community College, Editor of the Peace Studies Journal, National Co-coordinator of Save the Kids from Incarceration, Director of Academy for Peace Education, and Director of Outdoor Empowerment. Nocella is grounded in the fields of peace and conflict studies, justice studies, and education. Dr. Nocella has published more than 50 scholarly articles or book chapters and over 40 books; his most recent books include *From Education to Incarceration: Dismantling the School to Prison Pipeline* (Peter Lang Publishing 2014), *Educating for Action: Strategies to Ignite Social Justice* (New Society Press 2014), and *The End of Prisons: Reflections from the Decarceration Movement* (Rodopi 2013).

LUCAS ALAN DIETSCHE
Coordinator, Incarcerated Adults Support
lucasdietsche81@gmail.com

Lucas Alan Dietsche is currently pursuing his master's in criminology/criminal justice at the University of Wisconsin-Platteville. His master's thesis is on "Poetic Justice", using poetry for healing, dissuasion, and to help trauma-affected, system-involved youth. Currently living in Superior, Wisconsin he is self-taught poet and has published works such as *Word Out: Under the Big Top of Dodge and Stanley Correctional Facilities*, *Elba: Memoirs of an Ex-Capitalist*, *Commies and Zombies*, *Since the Oregon Trail*, *Moods are Like Wisconsin Weather*, and *Kapshida*. He has published poetry in *Transformative Justice Journal*, *Ariel Anthology*, and *Nemadji Review*. His blog is called "Xennial Poetry Notes." He was Superior's first Co-Poet Laureate, in 2019. Dietsche is the Regional Coordinator with Midwest Save the Kids from Incarceration, Formerly Incarcerated Peers, and organizer of Letters to Prisoners group. He has presented work on Letters to Prisoners, zines as radical pedagogy, and upon intersectionality.

JORDAN HALLIDAY

Designer

PinebeeCreative.com/contact

Jordan Halliday is the Founder & Creative Director of Pinebee Creative, an award-winning Creative Design Studio based in Salt Lake City, Utah. Jordan has assisted thousands of brands, both large and small, with creative design and development; from Disney, Nickelodeon, Carhartt, & Taco Bell, to local non-profits & small businesses. When not helping clients with their creative needs, Jordan also teaches Graphic Design & Web Development at Salt Lake Community College. Jordan is an activist, grand jury resister, and former political prisoner with a passion for prisoner support. Jordan sits on the board of many various non-profits, organizations, and committees.

RICARDO LEVINS MORALES

Cover Art

RLMartstudio.com

Based in Minneapolis, Ricardo Levins Morales is a social justice art warrior, speaker, and activist. He has long been involved in struggles for labor rights and social justice; he is currently active in the movement for police abolition. His creative images are widely used in schools, publications, organizing campaigns, and protests.

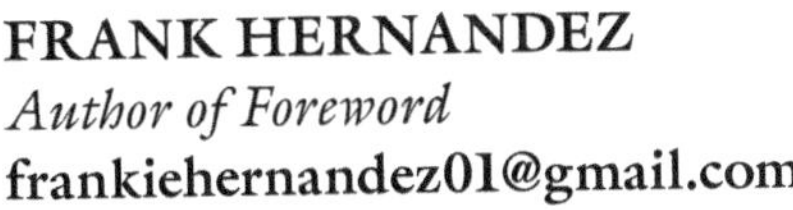

FRANK HERNANDEZ

Author of Foreword

frankiehernandez01@gmail.com

Frank Hernandez serves as Dean of the College of Education at TCU. Dr. Hernandez previously served as Associate Dean & The Harold and Annette Simmons Endowed Chair in Educational Policy and Leadership at the Simmons School of Education, Southern Methodist University. Dr. Hernandez' research work has focused on four areas of inquiry: Latinos and school leadership, Latino racial identity development, inclusive leadership for LGBTQ students, and leadership for social justice. He has published extensively on Latino leadership, including two books: *Abriendo Puertas, Cerrando Heridas (Opening Doors, Closing Wounds): Latinas/os Finding Work-Life Balance in Academia* (with Elizabeth Murakami and Gloria Rodriguez) and *Brown-Eyed Leaders of the Sun: A Portrait of Latina/o Educational Leaders* (with Elizabeth Murakami).

JONATHAN PAUL
Author of Preface
darkgreenradio@gmail.com

Jonathan Paul has been an activist since his late teens. In the mid-1980s, Jonathan traveled to California to join the animal rights movement. In 1997, Jonathan was one of the co-founders of the U.S. Hunt Saboteurs focused on disrupting trophy hunting of Bighorn Sheep, Bear, Bison, Tule Elk, Bison, and other wild species. Over the decades, Jonathan has founded Sea Defense Alliance, Ocean Defense International, America's Whale Alliance, Siskiyou Forest Defenders, Global Investigations, and is currently on the advisory board of Civil Liberties Defense Center. Jonathan was jailed for six months as a Grand Jury resister in 1992 and was in federal prison for 51 months for animal liberation activities in the late 1990s. Currently, Jonathan lives in Southern Oregon and does his podcast, Dark Green Radio, and continues to work on environmental and animal issues.

Anthony J. Nocella II, and Lea Lani Kinikini

Series Editors

Liberatory Stories and Voices from Community Colleges, an international peer-reviewed book series published by Peter Lang Publishing and co-edited by Dr. Anthony J. Nocella II and Dr. Lea Lani Kinikini, is a grass-roots community-focused radical transformative critical decolonizing anti-authoritarian book series on the political delineations of transforming education for liberation in communities occupying Indigenous territories and stolen land on Turtle Island (North America). This book series, supported by JEDI4ST, the interdisciplinary researcher center at Salt Lake Community College, will provide space and place for marginalized communities, students, staff, public intellectuals, activist-scholars, and frustrated administrators laboring in community colleges to critically resist and amplify their counter-stories which demand that in the rollout of the neoliberal corporate factory academic-industrial complex agenda, that public education must be affordable, inclusive, equitable, inclusive, just, transformative, and open to all. This book series foregrounds writer's agency with authentic story-telling, autoethnography, collective biography and life writing narratives and is a place for disseminating participatory action and social justice activist research. It seeks critical teaching and critical writing that resists Eurocentric pedagogies and methodologies such as denotative reports, standardized metrics and rubrics, corporate, neoliberal, capitalist, standardized, colonial, factory education that colonizes the mind. Instead, the series privileges radical liberatory praxis and makes space for outstanding embodied action research tied to teaching, transformative participatory projects created with not 'on' marginalized communities that centers the margin. Many of the students and faculty are at community colleges not merely because it is affordable, but moreover because community colleges defend political spaces for and with the oppressed: whether first generation (code for "working class"), the racially, territorially and marginalized 'others' that are pandemically silenced by repression and oppression. This series holds space and place that the community college is the last hope of democracy from which knowledge from and for the margins emerge as powerful countercurrents and disruptive discourses that liberate. This book series holds space and place for these voices who brave the world with knowledge in one hand and resistance in the other to liberate all.

For additional information about this series or for the submission of manuscripts, please contact:

Anthony J. Nocella II, Series Editor; nocellat@yahoo.com
Lea Lani Kinikini, Series Editor; lealani.kinikini@slcc.edu

To order other books in this series, please contact our Customer Service Department:

peterlang@presswarehouse.com (within the U.S.)
orders@peterlang.com (outside the U.S.)

Or browse online by series:
www.peterlang.com

www.ingramcontent.com/pod-product-compliance
Lightning Source LLC
Chambersburg PA
CBHW061719300426
44115CB00014B/2753

* 9 7 8 1 6 3 6 6 7 7 3 6 1 *